HISTORY & GEOGRAPH
A FARMING COMMU

MW00680131

CONTENTS

Author:	Mary Vandermey
Editor:	Richard W. Wheeler, M.A.Ed.
Consulting Editor:	Howard Stitt, Th.M., Ed.D.
Revision Editor:	Alan Christopherson, M.S.

Alpha Omega Publications®

804 N. 2nd Ave. E., Rock Rapids, IA 51246-1759

Learn with our friends:

When you see me, I will help your teacher explain the exciting things you are expected to do.

When you do actions with me, you will learn how to write, draw, match words, read, and much more.

You and I will learn about matching words, listening, drawing, and other fun things in your lessons.

A FARMING COMMUNITY

This LIFEPAC® is about a wheat farm in Kansas. You will meet Judie and Paul who visit this farm. You will read about their trip around the state. You will learn about the early people who lived there. You will find out how a church helped a little boy. Before the visit is over, you will know much about the state of Kansas.

 **Objectives**

Read these objectives. They will tell you what you will be able to do when you have finished this LIFEPAC.

1. You will be able to tell how people raise wheat.
2. You will be able to name the six sections of Kansas and to tell in what way each one is special.
3. You will be able to tell how the early settlers lived.
4. You will be able to locate Kansas on the map.
5. You will be able to tell how a church helped a boy.
6. You will be able to locate the center of the parts of the United States that touch.

NEW WORDS

bale. To tie up in bundles.

capital (cap i tal). The city in which the work of a state is done.

chalk. A soft, white stone.

clay. Earth that can be shaped when wet.

coal. A hard, black substance that can burn.

collection (col lec tion). A group of things.

combine (com bine). A machine that cuts and threshes grain and other crops.

crutch. A support to help a person walk.

disk. A farm tool used to break up plowed ground.

elevator (el e va tor). A building for storing grain.

evaporate (e vap o rate). To remove the water from something.

geographical (ge o graph i cal). About the surface of a country.

grandparents (grand par ents). Both grandmother and grandfather.

grind. To crush into powder.

hail. Frozen drops of water.

harrow (har row). A farm tool used to smooth out plowed ground.

harvest (har vest). To gather the ripe grain.

hunch. A hump.

invasion (in va sion). An entering by force.

kirk. A Scottish word meaning church.

library (li brar y). A building with books to use.

mission (mis sion). A place where God's Word is told to people.

monster (mon ster). A large make-believe animal.

operation (op er a tion). The surgical repair made by a doctor.

petroglyph (pet ro glyph). A picture word found on a rock.

pew. A seat in a church.

pioneer (pi o neer). An early settler.

prairie (prair ie). A flat, grassy land.

preserve (pre serve). A place to keep animals safe.

President (pres i dent). The leader of a country.

range. Grassland used to feed cattle.

scroll. A roll of parchment or paper.

section (sec tion). A part of something.

shark. A large ocean fish.

silo (si lo). A tall round building in which green food for animals is stored.

sod. Earth and grass together.

strip mining (strip min ing). The digging of coal from the top of the ground.

successful (suc cess ful). Winning.

tablet (tab let). A flat piece of stone or clay used to write on.

thresh. To take the seeds off the grain stems.

wheat. A grain used for flour.

These words will appear in **boldface** (darker print) the first time they are used.

I. FLYING INTO KANSAS

Are you ready to travel along with Judie and Paul? They have been flying from Maine today. They are almost ready to land in Kansas. Fasten your seat belt!

capital	(cap i tal)	The city in which the work of a state is done.
grandparents	(grand par ents)	Both grandmother and grandfather.
hail		Frozen drops of water.
operation	(op er a tion)	The cutting of someone by a doctor.
pioneer	(pi o neer)	An early settler.
section	(sec tion)	A part of something.
silo	(si lo)	A tall round building in which green food for animals is stored.
wheat		A grain used for flour.

Ask your teacher to say these words with you.
Teacher check _____

               Initial   Date

There is a blank Kansas map on the next page and a larger one on page 57. As you read this LIFEPAC about Kansas you will be told what to mark on your map.

You will need these things for the map activities in this LIFEPAC:

    your map of Kansas on page 57
    one black pen   one blue pen
    one red pen   one green pen

☐ Use the black pen for the highways on which they traveled.

☐ Use the red pen to print names of places.

☐ Use the blue pen for names of things they saw.

☐ Use the green pen for names of parts of the state, or other states.

Put a check in the box after you do each map activity.

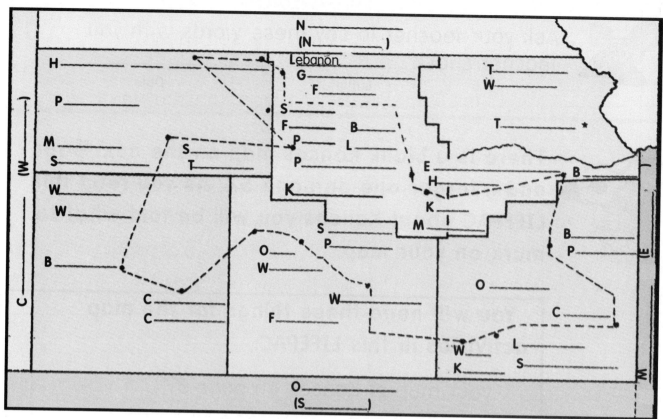

Your Map of Kansas
Map 1

A SUMMER VACATION

Judie and Paul looked out of the window from the plane. They were flying over Kansas now.

"Look!" said Judie. "Look at all the fields! Black strips run between some of the fields."

"I see cars moving on those black strips!" said Paul.

"And I see houses, barns, and a river!" said Judie.

A voice said, "Please fasten your seat belts. We will be landing in Topeka (to pe ka), Kansas, in five minutes."

Judie and Paul fastened their seat belts. Their trip was almost over.

Judie and Paul lived in Maine. Their father was a fisherman. Ever since they could remember they had been saying, "Our **grandparents** live on a farm in Kansas. Someday we will visit them."

The plane slowed down. Just below lay the airport runway. The plane touched ground with a little bump.

Soon they saw Grandfather waving to them. "Hello, Judie! Hello, Paul!" he called.

"Grandfather!" said Judie and Paul at the same time. They rushed to him. He held them close.

"Did you have a good plane ride?" he asked.

"It was wonderful!" said Judie.

Do this map activity.

1.1   Judie and Paul flew to Topeka, Kansas.
☐ Label Topeka in red on your map.

Teacher check _____
                Initial   Date

Grandfather said, "After we pick up your bags, we will be on our way to my farm near Lebanon (le ba non). We will ride in my camper."

"We will drive into Topeka before we go to the farm," said Grandfather. "The work of running the state goes on there. Topeka is the **capital** of Kansas."

"Why didn't Grandmother come with you?" asked Judie.

"She had a meeting at the church," Grandfather said. "She is helping to plan a dinner to earn money to help a boy."

"Why does he need help?" Paul asked.

Grandfather said, "His name is David. You

Do this map activity.

1.2   Judie and Paul flew over many states.

☐ Label in green on your map the states which border Kansas.

☐ Label in black North, South, East, and West on your map. Turn a few pages to look at Grandfather's map for help.

Teacher check _____
                Initial   Date

will meet him. He lives with his grandmother on the farm next to us. David needs an **operation**. The church people will help her pay for the operation."

As they drove along, Grandfather said, "Those clouds look like rain."

"How can you tell?" asked Judie.

"A black cloud rolling in the west sometimes means rain and wind."

"Our clouds in Maine come mostly from the east. They come from the Atlantic Ocean," said Paul.

"Farmers don't mind gentle rains," said Grandfather. "But they don't want wind and **hail**. Hail can hurt a crop in five minutes."

Grandfather pointed to a green field. "See that wheat? That's winter wheat. We plant winter wheat in the fall. This wheat is called Red Turkey. The wheat is made into **flour**. The flour makes good bread."

The black clouds piled higher in the sky. The wind began to make the camper sway. A gentle rain began to fall.

Grandfather said, "Kansas winds blow hard. Here on flat land nothing stops the wind."

"This rain was a gift from God," said Grandfather. "I give thanks. The wheat needs this gentle rain. I call it a soaker."

"What does that mean?" asked Paul.

"It means," said Grandfather, "that the rain soaks into the ground. It doesn't run off like a hard rain does."

Judie and Paul grew more excited during the ride. Finally, there was the farm! They saw a white house and red barns. They saw a giant round building which grandfather said was a **silo**.

Grandmother called and waved. Judie and Paul ran to her. "Grandmother, we're here!" they yelled.

They saw land stretching as far as they could see. Maine was so different. Because of the hills in Maine, they couldn't see far. But, the Kansas fields were bright green with growing wheat. They saw cows and horses feeding in a far pasture.

 You have already learned a lot about Kansas. **Choose a word from the Word Box to finish the sentence.**

1.3   Judie and Paul took a trip by _____.

1.4   They live in _____.

1.5   They visited the state of _____.

1.6   Gentle rains are called _____.

1.7   The main crop in Kansas is _____.

		Word Box
1.8	Crops are hurt by _____.	soakers
1.9	One kind of wheat is _____	camper
	_____.	flat
1.10	Winter wheat is planted in the	Kansas
	_____.	wheat
1.11	The land in Kansas is very	plane
	_____.	hail
1.12	Judie, Paul, and Grandfather rode	fall
	in a _____.	Red Turkey
		Maine

THE SIX PARTS OF KANSAS

Grandmother said, "David is coming over tomorrow. You can play in the dugout (dug out). He wants to see you."

"What is a dugout?" said Paul. "It sounds like a cave."

"Wait. You will be surprised," said Grandmother.

Grandfather put a piece of paper on the table. On the paper Grandfather drew a map of Kansas. He said, "Kansas is divided into six parts. I'll mark them out on the map."

While Judie and Paul watched, he drew some lines.

Grandfather said, "Here in the northeast is Trails West. It was named when only trails were this way. No roads were in it then."

"This," he said, "is the Big Lake part. Judie, what do you think that means?"

"Big lakes are in it," Judie said.

"Right! Now, next comes the Pioneer **section**. The people who came here first were the **pioneers**. This section is in the northwest. Big wheat fields are here."

Grandfather drew another section. "In the southwest we have the Wild West section."

Paul said, "That's where the cowboys are!"

"Right again!" Grandfather marked out two more sections. "These sections in the south are Frontier (Fron tier) and Ozark (o zark). The Ozark section is near the Ozark Mountains of Missouri (mis sour i)," he told Judie and Paul. "Wait until you see the salt plant in the Frontier section!" he said.

"A salt plant?" asked Judie and Paul together.

 **Kansas is divided into six parts. Write the six sections here.** The names are in the story. The first letter of each word is given for you.

1.13   T _____   W _____

1.14   B _____   L _____

1.15   P _____

1.16   W _____   W _____

1.17   F _____

1.18   O _____

Do this map activity.

1.19   This is Grandfather's map. Mark and label
        your map so that it looks like Grandfather's.

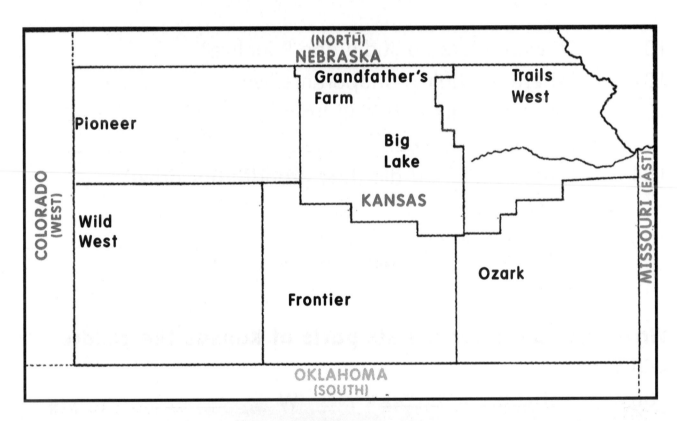

Grandfather's Map
Map 2

Teacher check _____
                    Initial   Date

13 (thirteen)

Review
REVIEW
Review

For this Self Test, study what you have read and done. The Self Test will check what you remember.

Self Test 1

Write the correct answers to these questions. Write your answers in the blanks.

1.01   In what state do Judie and Paul live? _____

1.02   Where do their grandparents live? _____

1.03   How did Judie and Paul travel to Kansas?_____
_____

1.04   What kind of car did their grandfather drive?
_____

1.05   What is the name of a kind of wheat? _____
_____

Write the names for the six parts of Kansas the children will visit.

1.06   T _____   W_____

1.07   B _____   L _____

1.08   P _____

1.09   W_____   W_____

1.010   F _____

1.011   O _____

From the list choose the names of the four states which border Kansas.

1.012 _____   Colorado

1.013 _____   Oregon

1.014 _____   Missouri

1.015 _____   Nebraska

                                                                Oklahoma

                                                                 Pennsylvania

                                                                 Maine

Write true **or** false.

1.016 _____ Judie and Paul's grandparents live in a city.

1.017 _____ Cowboys are in the Wild West part of Kansas.

1.018 _____ A soaker is a heavy rain.

1.019 _____ Winter wheat is planted in the fall.

1.020 _____ The land in Kansas is very hilly.

1.021 _____ The children could not see far in Kansas.

1.022 _____ Judie and Paul saw lions and zebras eating grass.

1.023 _____ Hail is good for plants.

1.024 _____ Florida is beside Kansas on the north.

1.025 _____ Kansas has six parts.

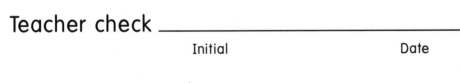

Teacher check _____

                          Initial   Date

20 / 25

EACH ANSWER, 1 POINT

My Score

II. GETTING TO KNOW KANSAS

Did you enjoy the ride to the big farm? Are you ready to look around the farm? Do you want to meet David? Grandfather will have some good stories to tell Judie and Paul. Let's go!

geographical	(ge o graph i cal)	About the surface of a country.
invasion	(in va sion)	An entering by force.
sod		Earth and grass together.

Ask your teacher to say these words with you. Teacher check _____

Initial   Date

SODDIES AND DUGOUTS

David came early the next morning. He walked slowly.

Judie, David, and Paul were friends right away.

"I'll show you the dugout," David said. He led the way. They walked slowly together.

He said, "I'll be glad when I have the operation.

Then I will be able to run like other people. I am glad there are Christians to help me. They live as Jesus taught. I want to help people sometime, too."

It was dark and cold inside the dugout.

David said, "The first people who came here didn't have houses. There were no big trees for wooden houses.

"So the men dug a square hole in the ground. They put poles cut from thin trees over the hole. Next they put branches over the poles. Then they put dirt over the branches. The dugout had only one door, and no windows. But the people were protected from cold and rain and wild animals."

"I think they knew God would help them, too," said Judie.

David told them that people learned to make a half-dugout later. The half-dugout had a half-wall, and a window.

Draw a picture of a dugout. Read the words about a dugout again. Make your picture as if you could see the inside and top at the same time.

Teacher check _____

                         Initial   Date

Kansas has six parts. Each part is named for a special reason. Match the part of Kansas with the reason.

2.1	Trails West	pioneers settled
2.2	Big Lakes	ocean beaches
2.3	Pioneer Section	only trails
24	Wild West	salt plant
2.5	Frontier	cowboys
2.6	Ozark	large lakes
		mountains

A Sod House

"Later on, the people built **sod** houses," David said. "The new homes were called Soddies (sod dies)."

In spring after the snow was gone, the ground was soft. The people cut the sod into long bricks. The best sod had short, thick grass in it. The grass held the earth together.

The builders left two holes in the walls for a window and a door. The floors were dirt. During a hard rain, water came through the roof.

Early people in Kansas made three kinds of homes. Under the homes write the words that tell about them.

1 window	no windows	part of a wall
1 door	1 door	underground
grass and earth	1 window	above ground
1 door		

2.7   **Dugout**   **Half-Wall**   **Soddy**

_____   _____   _____

_____   _____   _____

_____   _____   _____

_____   _____   _____

LEBANON, GEOGRAPHICAL CENTER OF THE UNITED STATES

Next day Grandmother and Grandfather took the children for a short ride. "You are going to see the **geographical** center of the parts of the United States that touch," Grandfather told them.

"What is that?" asked Paul.

Judie said, "I think it is the middle of the United States."

"Right!" said Grandfather.

Near the town of Lebanon stood a stone marker. The flag of the United States flew from the top. They stood and looked at it. Grandmother said that they were in the geographical center of the states that touch.

Do this map activity.

> **You will need these things to mark your map:**
>   **red pen**   **United States map**

Check the box after you do each step.

☐ Draw a line from the state marked Washington to the one marked Florida.

☐ Draw a line from New York to Los Angeles, California. The lines should cross near Lebanon. You have found the geographical center of the parts of the United States that touch.

Teacher check _____
                    Initial   Date

Listen to the long /i/ sound in the word mice. **Circle each word below that has the long /i/ sound.**

2.8

kind	child	silk	mild
milk	ring	wild	kick
inch	mind	bind	pink

As they rode back to the farm, a huge grasshopper hit the car.

Grandfather said, "Let me tell you about our famous grasshopper **invasion**."

"One day about one hundred years ago there wasn't a cloud in the sky. About 4 o'clock the sky grew dark.

"Suddenly out of the northwest came a terrible buzzing sound. Millions of grasshoppers flew in. They hit the ground, covering everything.

"Grasshoppers fell into the streams. The water turned brown.

"The chickens tried to eat the grasshoppers. They ate until they were stuffed. But the chickens couldn't eat all of the grasshoppers.

"The grasshoppers ate the corn. They ate straw hats. They ate things of leather. They ate the wooden handles of tools. Inside houses, they ate curtains. The crops were gone. The people had very little left. People had to help each other."

After the story, Judie said, "I'm glad we don't have that many grasshoppers in Maine. We do have fogs that are bad. But people help each other if they are caught out in the fog and can't see."

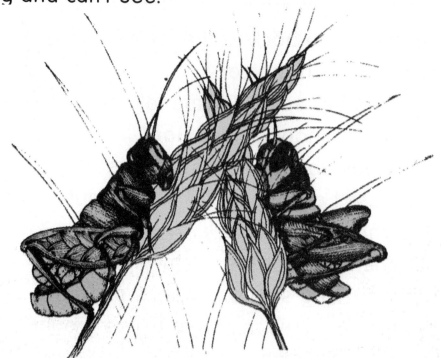

Grasshoppers invaded Kansas.

Grandfather said, "Kansas is called the Breadbasket of the nation because we raise so much wheat here.

"But crops were not always good," Grandfather told them. "Some years there was no rain. The winds blew. The winds carried dust high into the sky. The crops died. Kansas was called the Dust Bowl then. Many farmers had to go to other states to live."

As they passed another wheat field, Grandfather said, "Many farmers use the same crop two times. In spring when the wheat is about four inches high, the farmers let their cattle in to eat. Then, they take the cattle out and let the wheat grow up again. The wheat plants grow thicker this time."

They saw many tall plants with large yellow flowers.

"What are those flowers?" asked Judie.

David said, "Those are sunflowers (sun flow ers). The sunflower is the state flower of

Sunflowers grow in Kansas.

Kansas. It grows when there is rain. It grows without rain. Even grasshoppers will not eat sunflowers."

They saw fields of tall corn, too.

At home later, Grandmother said, "Tonight we are going to the church supper. The church members want to earn more money for David's operation."

Judie and Paul felt proud to be a part of helping David. He had become their best friend.

Find an encyclopedia that will help you with these tasks. Use paper from your classroom. Put a check in the box when you do that step.

☐ Draw and color the Kansas state flower.

☐ Draw and color the Kansas state flag.

☐ Draw and color the Kansas state bird.

☐ Draw and color the Kansas state tree.

☐ Read to find out why each of these was chosen.

Teacher check _____
　　　　　　　　　Initial　　　　　　　　　　　Date

Judie and Paul have seen many different things in Kansas. Answer these questions with yes **or** no.

2.9   Did Grandfather live in Topeka, Kansas?＿＿＿＿＿＿＿

2.10   Is the Kansas state flower the sunflower?＿＿＿＿＿＿＿

2.11   Is the geographical center of the parts of the United
        States that touch near Lebanon, Kansas?＿＿＿＿＿＿

2.12   Can wheat grow after cattle eat off the tops?＿＿＿＿＿

2.13   Did grasshoppers eat all the crops in Kansas once?＿＿＿

2.14   When it doesn't rain, are there dust storms in Kansas?

        ＿＿＿＿＿＿＿＿

2.15   Do the strong winds in Kansas help the farmer?＿＿＿＿

2.16   Is bread made from sunflowers?＿＿＿＿＿＿＿＿

2.17   When Kansas had no rain was it called the Dust Bowl?

        ＿＿＿＿＿＿＿

2.18   Is Kansas known as the Breadbasket of the nation?

        ＿＿＿＿＿＿＿

Review
REVIEW
Review

For this Self Test, study what you have read and done. This Self Test will check what you remember of this part and other parts you have read.

Self Test 2

Put X in front of the best answer.

2.01   Dugouts are   ＿＿＿＿＿ a. tents.

                                          ＿＿＿＿＿ b. caves.

                                          ＿＿＿＿＿ c. nests.

2.02   Sod houses are made of   ＿＿＿＿ a. soil and grass.

                                          ＿＿＿＿＿ b. wood.

                                          ＿＿＿＿＿ c. bricks.

2.03   Lebanon, Kansas, is   _____ a. an island.

_____ b. a river.

_____ c. the center of the parts of the United States that touch.

2.04   Farmers do not like to see _____ a. storm clouds.

_____ b. highways.

_____ c. tall trees.

2.05   Judie and Paul went on a trip.   _____ a. to the United States.

_____ b. to Maine.

_____ c. to Kansas.

Write true **or** false.

2.06   _____   Grandfather lived on a farm in Kansas.

2.07   _____   Once flocks of birds came and ate the farmers' crops.

2.08   _____   When there is no rain in Kansas, dust storms may come.

2.09   _____   The state flower of Kansas is the sunflower.

2.010   _____   Lebanon, Kansas, is the geographical center of the parts of the United States that touch.

2.011   _____   Some farmers let their cattle eat the wheat tops in the spring.

2.012   _____   The farmers do not get a wheat crop if the cattle eat it first.

2.013 _____ The children took a trip around Kansas on a train.

2.014 _____ A dust bowl is used by Grandmother when she cooks.

Name the six sections of Kansas.

2.015 _____

2.016 _____

2.017 _____

2.018 _____

2.019 _____

2.020 _____

Circle the right answer. Write the word in the blank.

2.021　Topeka is a city in _____.

　　　　　　　Maine　　　　　　　Kansas

2.022　A soddy was _____ ground.

　　　　　　　below　　　　　　　above

2.023　Kansas is very _____.

　　　　　　　flat　　　　　　　hilly

2.024　The Breadbasket of the nation is_____.

　　　　　　　Maine　　　　　　　Kansas

2.025　A name of winter wheat is _____ Turkey.

　　　　　　　Red　　　　　　　Blue

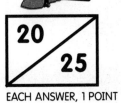

Teacher check _____

　　　　　　　　　　　Initial　　　　　　　Date

20 / 25

EACH ANSWER, 1 POINT

My Score

III. EXPLORING KANSAS

You are really having a busy time with Judie, Paul, and David.

Grandfather has told some interesting stories. Now, he and Grandmother are ready to take the three children around Kansas. You know they will visit some exciting places. You want to know about Kansas, too, so hurry up!

bale		To tie up in bundles.
chalk		A soft, white stone.
clay		Earth that can be shaped when wet.
coal		A hard, black substance that can burn.
collection	(col lec tion)	A group of things.
combine	(com bine)	A machine that cuts and threshes grain and other crops.

HISTORY & GEOGRAPHY

302

LIFEPAC TEST

22 / 28

Name _____

Date _____

Score _____

HISTORY & GEOGRAPHY 302: LIFEPAC TEST

EACH ANSWER, 1 POINT

Answer true **or** false.

1. _____ Kansas at one time was an ocean.
2. _____ Judie and Paul's grandparents lived in Nebraska.
3. _____ Lebanon, Kansas, is the geographical center of the parts of the United States that touch.
4. _____ Kansas is called the Breadbasket of the nation.
5. _____ There were only trees in the State Game Preserves.
6. _____ The state flower of Kansas is the sunflower.
7. _____ Combines cut and thresh the wheat.
8. _____ Trucks take the threshed wheat to gas stations.
9. _____ Kansas was named for the Big Lake Indians.
10. _____ The children's grandfather owned a factory.

Put X **beside the word in the second column that goes with the word in the first column.**

11. Red Turkey wheat is _____ a. winter wheat.
    _____ b. summer wheat.
    _____ c. spring wheat.

12. soddies

_____ a. wood and paper

_____ b. cement and rock

_____ c. soil and grass

13. petroglyphs

_____ a. English

_____ b. Indian

_____ c. German

14. After harvesting, fields are

_____ a. left alone.

_____ b. used for rodeos.

_____ c. plowed.

15. The capital of Kansas is

_____ a. Ottawa.

_____ b. Lebanon.

_____ c. Topeka.

16. Buffalo in Kansas live on

_____ a. farms.

_____ b. mountains.

_____ c. preserves.

17. Kansas dust storms come in

_____ a. winter.

_____ b. dry weather.

_____ c. rainy weather.

18. Kansas grows

_____ a. cotton.

_____ b. wheat.

_____ c. sugar cane.

19.   cowboy capital   _____   a. Lebanon
                        _____   b. Hutchinson
                        _____   c. Dodge City

20.   Crops were once   _____   a. birds.
      eaten by   _____   b. snakes.
                        _____   c. grasshoppers.

Circle the right answer.

21.   God's animals are saved in _____.
      preserves   presents   reserves

22.   Wheat is stored in _____.
      elevators   garages   houses

23.   Wheat is ground into _____.
      paste   flour   seeds

24.   The first settlers lived in _____.
      houses   dugouts   cabins

25.   Coal is mined by _____ in Kansas.
      shaft mining   closed mining   strip mining

Answer these questions.

26.   Why did the settlers build stone fence posts?
      _____

27.   What do black rolling clouds often mean in Kansas?
      _____

28.   Why are wheat growers afraid of hail storms in
      summer? _____

      _____

elevator	(el e va tor)	A building for storing grain.
evaporate	(e vap o rate)	To remove the water from something.
hunch		A hump.
kirk		A Scottish word meaning church.
library	(li brar y)	A building with books to use.
mission	(mis sion)	A place where God's Word is told to people.
petroglyph	(pet ro glyph)	A picture word found on a rock.
pew		A seat in a church.
prairie	(prair ie)	A flat, grassy land.
preserve	(pre serve)	A place to keep animals safe.
president	(pres i dent)	The leader of a country.
range		Grassland used to feed cattle.
scroll		A roll of parchment or paper.

shark		A large ocean fish.
strip mining (strip min ing)		The digging of coal from the top of the ground.
tablet	(tab let)	A flat piece of stone or clay used to write on.
thresh		To take the seeds off the grain stems.

 Ask your teacher to say these words with you. Teacher check _____

Initial   Date

A SONG AND SOME BUFFALO

The trip through Kansas had just started. Grandfather, Grandmother, and the three children were in the camper. They stopped first to visit the cabin of Dr. Brewster (brew ster) Higley (hig ley) in Smith Center. Dr. Higley wrote the words for Home on the Range (**range**) over one hundred years ago. For the rest of the trip, everyone sang that song more than any other song.

After seeing the old cabin, Grandfather said they would go to see some things that were even older at Horsethief (horse thief) Canyon (can yon).

The children were surprised to see the pictures painted on the walls of the canyon. Grandfather explained that the pictures were called **petroglyphs**. The pictures were paintings done by early Indians. The pictures told a story without using letters and words. Grandfather told them that many Indians had lived in Kansas.

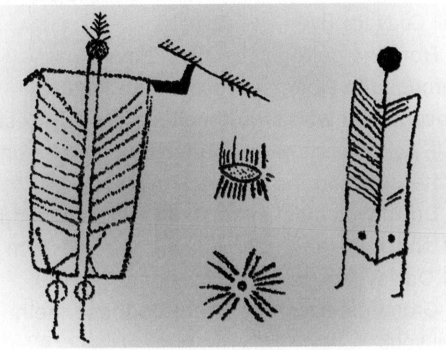

The pictures tell a story.

Write a story using your own petroglyphs.

Teacher check _____

Initial   Date

Judie wanted to remember all she saw. She wrote down what her grandfather told her about each place. Grandmother helped her with the spelling. Judie wrote,

"In Hays I saw twenty-seven markers in honor of western people. Some of them were Wild Bill Hickok (hick ok) and General (gen er al) George Custer (cus ter) and Buffalo Bill Cody (co dy)."

From the petroglyphs, they drove west through the Pioneer section. The land became dry with strange **chalk** forms. These tall, pointed hills were formed by the wind and water wearing the soft rock away.

David was most interested in the thousands of **shark** teeth that they saw in the museum at Oakley (oak ley).

Grandfather asked, "What do these teeth tell you?"

"I know!" said Paul. "This land was once an ocean. It would have been during and after the Flood of Noah's day. But then the ocean dried up and the sharks died."

"Right!" said Grandfather.

As they drove on they could see Mount Sunflower in the distance. It seemed so high, because most of Kansas is flat.

Do this map activity.

In the Pioneer section, everyone could see very far.
☐ Trace with black the trip from the farm through the Pioneer section.

☐ Label with blue: a. Home on the Range
b. petroglyphs
c. shark's teeth

☐ Label in red Mount Sunflower.

Teacher check _____

Initial   Date

Next the children visited the State Game **Preserve** in the Wild West section. Many animals could be seen.

David said, "These are God's animals. We should take care of them."

The children stood at the high wire fence. The wild buffalo (buf fa lo) had huge **hunched** backs. The animals tossed their heads and looked at their visitors.

Grandfather said, "Once, thousands of buffalo lived on these plains. But people killed them for their hides. Soon, something

33 (thirty-three)

had to be done to save the buffalo. They were put in preserves to be safe.

Paul said, "In Maine fishermen have to scoop fish up in little nets. They cannot catch too many fish at one time."

The children saw other animals. They saw beavers (bea vers) at work building dams. Deer and elk were walking around. Many birds were flying overhead.

They drove on to Dodge City. Judie, Paul, and David enjoyed walking along the cowboy part of the town. The buildings looked very old but were really copies of old buildings. They learned that Dodge City is called the Cowboy Capital of the World.

Grandfather explained, "At one time millions of cattle were driven from Texas. They were put on the trains here and sent to other parts of the country to market."

Do this map activity.

Everyone liked the Wild West section.

- [ ] Label in blue the buffalo.

- [ ] Label the Cowboy Capital on your map in red.

- [ ] Trace in black their trip into the Wild West section on your map.

Teacher check _____

                         Initial   Date

OIL WELLS AND SALT

The trip continued. They had reached the Frontier section. "Many things are going on in this part of Kansas," said Grandfather.

"What are those?" asked Paul. Everyone turned to look where he pointed.

35 (thirty-five)

"Those are oil wells," said Grandmother.

They saw huge pumps with their arms going up and down. The pumps were drawing oil from the ground.

"It's strange to see oil wells close to wheat fields," said Judie.

The next day at Hutchinson (hutch in son) they visited the largest salt plant in the world.

Grandfather explained, "First the salt is dug up. Then the salt is cleaned. Next the water is **evaporated**. What is left is the salt you use."

Kansas seemed to be filled with the largest of everything! They saw the largest grain **elevator** in the world.

At Wichita they saw where airplanes were being built.

They saw great flour mills where wheat was ground. They saw large meat packing plants.

"Kansas has just about everything!" said Paul.

Do this map activity.

There were so many things to see in the Frontier section.

☐ Trace the trip in black through the Frontier section.

☐ Label in red Wichita.

☐ Label in blue the salt plant and oil wells.

Teacher check _____
                        Initial   Date

They drove on from Wichita into the Ozark section.

In Cedar Vale (ce dar vale) they saw something they would never forget. It was a tiny church called Wee **Kirk** of The Valley.

Inside the church were just six **pews**. Each pew held only two people. They thanked God for the beautiful world He had made.

Grandfather explained, "Those twelve seats stand for the twelve disciples of Jesus."

Later, as David was telling about reading a book about **prairie** life, they drove up to a schoolhouse near Independence (in de pen dence). A sign said that the stories about the early settlers happened near here.

"This is the most exciting part of the trip," said David. "My grandmother read a lot of the books about the Kansas family to me. I can't run and play so I spend a lot of time reading."

Their next stop was in Pittsburg. The land has more hills now. As they rode along, they saw **coal** being dug out of the ground. The **strip mining** has left ugly hills and ditches.

"The people have been kind to God's land. They have planted trees and grass so that the ugly hills would be pretty again," said Grandmother.

Do this map activity.

Grandmother and Grandfather saw many things in the Ozark section.

☐ Trace in black the trip into the Ozark section.

☐ Label in blue
    a. Wee Kirk
    b. little schoolhouse
    c. coal

Teacher check _____
                Initial   Date

They went north from Pittsburg. In Humboldt (hum boldt), they heard about the Bible parade held every year in October. People make floats of stories from the Bible. Judie and Paul were sorry they would have to go home before the parade.

Draw a picture of the float you would like to have in the Bible parade.

Teacher check _____

Initial   Date

OLD BIBLES AND FENCE POSTS

They drove north into the Trails West section. Judie wrote a lot of notes on the Bible **collection** they saw at Baldwin (bald win).

"I want to tell about these old books and **scrolls** in Sunday school when I go back to Maine," said Judie.

They looked at the **clay tablets** from early Bible times, old scrolls, old written Bibles, and a piece of a very famous printed Bible.

Do this map activity.

Judie, Paul, and, David have been visiting in Trails West.

☐ Mark in black on your map the trip through the Trails West section.

☐ Label in blue the Bible Parade.

☐ Print the word Bible in blue where the Bible collection is kept.

Teacher check _____

Initial   Date

As they drove into the Big Lake section they talked about the early plains Indians.

"We will soon see an Indian school," said Grandmother.

At Council Grove (coun cil grove) they saw the Kaw **Mission**, a Christian school for Indian children. "This is an old school," Grandmother told them.

Grandfather said, "The state of Kansas was named after the Kansa (kan sa) Indians. Many Indian tribes have lived here."

As they rode along later, they enjoyed looking at the lakes and pretty land.

"Are a lot of game preserves in Kansas?" asked Paul.

"Yes, we try to help our animal friends. We have made places for them to live safely," answered Grandfather.

As they drove on, Grandmother told them about Abilene (ab i lene), the next town.

"Abilene is an important town," said Grandmother. "One of our **Presidents**, Dwight Eisenhower (eis en how er), lived here when he was your age." They passed the plain house where the President had lived. They visited the **library** and museum. They went inside the church he had attended.

Do this map activity.

Your friends are visiting the Big Lake part of Kansas.

- ☐ Mark the trip in black.

- ☐ Label in red the Kaw Mission and Eisenhower home.

Teacher check _____
              Initial   Date

That night Grandfather told them, "Tomorrow we will see the famous stone fence posts of Kansas."

Next morning, as they drove toward the farm, they saw the stone fence posts. They were wider at the bottom than at the top. The fence wire went between the posts.

Grandfather told them about the posts. "Early settlers were the first to use stone fence posts. There were not enough trees to cut for wooden posts. The stone was dug from the ground."

Read these words. Write the correct word in each sentence.

sprinkle	spring	shrine
shrill	shrink	spread

3.1   The church was like a _____.

3.2   The corn did not _____ but it grew taller.

3.3   A soaker rain lasts longer than a _____ of rain.

3.4   The wild bird had a _____ call.

3.5   The green fields _____ for miles and miles.

3.6   In the _____ the strong winds blow.

Do this map activity.

The trip in Big Lake was the last part of the trip around Kansas.

☐ Mark in black the trip back to the farm.

☐ Label in blue the stone fence posts.

Teacher check _____
Initial   Date

This would be David's last trip before his operation. He said, "I can hardly wait. I want to walk like other people. Every night I say, 'Thank you, God, for nice people to help me.' "

Grandfather said, "Any day the **combines** will start to work. The combines cut and thresh the wheat. Then the straw will be baled."

"What does **bale** mean?" asked Judie.

"It means to tie the straw in bundles after the wheat is taken off the tops."

Draw lines to match.

3.7	Indian writings	bale
3.8	dried up	combine
3.9	where animals are safe	preserve
3.10	to tie straw in bundles	ocean in Kansas
3.11	famous cowboy	conservation
3.12	cuts and threshes	Buffalo Bill
3.13	saving God's world	petroglyphs

Teacher check _____

Review
REVIEW
Review

Study what you have read and done for this Self Test. This Self Test will check what you remember of this part and other parts you have read.

SELF TEST 3

Mark T **for** true **and** F **for** false.

3.01 _____ Lebanon, Kansas, is the geographical center of the parts of the United States that touch.

3.02 _____ The pioneers used stone fence posts because they had no wood.

3.03 _____ In strip mining coal is mined by digging it out of the ground.

3.04 _____ Many famous fishermen have lived in Dodge City.

3.05 _____ Gentle rains are called lazy rains.

Circle the right answer. Print the word in the blank.

3.06 In the Wild West area there are many _____ .

      airplanes   cowboys   doctors

3.07 The state flower is the _____ .

      sunflower   pansy   rose

3.08 Kansas is called the Breadbasket of the nation because a lot of _____ is raised.

wheat   grass   flour

3.09 _____ is known for its cowboys.

Ford City   Honda City   Dodge City

3.010 The capital of Kansas is _____.

Topeka   Lebanon   Wichita

3.011 The geographical center of the parts of the United States that touch is near _____.

Topeka   Lebanon   Wichita

3.012 Early homes in Kansas were _____.

soddies   grassies   dirties

3.013 Animals are safe in the _____.

reserves   conserves   preserves

Match the following parts of Kansas to something you could see in each part.

3.014	Trails West	cowboys
3.015	Big Lake	strip mining
3.016	Pioneer	salt plant
3.017	Wild West	farms and lakes
3.018	Frontier	Mount Sunflower
3.019	Ozark	clay tablets

Write your answer.

3.020 Write about the part of the visit to Kansas by Judie and Paul that you like best. _____

_____

_____

_____

_____

_____

_____

_____

Teacher check _____

Initial   Date

16 / 20

EACH ANSWER, 1 POINT

My Score

IV. HARVESTING IN KANSAS

Are you rested from the big trip around Kansas? Judie, Paul, and David had a good time, too. The day for David's operation will soon be here. The wheat is ready to be **harvested.** How busy everyone is on a farm! Summer will soon be over. Read on. Enjoy the last of Judie and Paul's summer in Kansas.

crutch		A support to help a person walk.
disk		A farm tool used to break up plowed ground.
grind		To crush into powder.
harrow	(har row)	A farm tool used to smooth out plowed ground.
harvest	(har vest)	To gather the ripe grain.
monster	(mon ster)	A large, make-believe animal.
successful	(suc cess ful)	Winning.

Ask your teacher to say these words with you.
Teacher check _____
Initial   Date

COMBINES AT WORK

As they reached the farm, Grandfather said, "The wheat is ready to harvest. Look! It's like growing gold!"

"When will you cut it?" asked Judie.

"Tomorrow the combines are to be here."

The wheat did look like gold as it waved in the wind.

Grandfather said, "I say a prayer of thanks for that ripe wheat. This time of year a farmer holds his breath. He watches the sky. He listens to weather news. He prays a lot."

Some light clouds were in the sky. Judie asked, "Do those clouds look bad?"

Grandfather said, "No. The black rolling clouds are the bad ones. Hail could spoil the year's work in five minutes."

Early the next morning the combines arrived. The huge machines went into the wheat fields. A line of trucks followed them. One truck at a time went beside each combine. The truck caught the wheat pouring out of the combine.

Judie and Paul watched excitedly. But David had seen it all before.

Write the right prefix before each word below.

a-   in-   dis-

4.1   Grandfather helped the children _____ cover the six parts of Kansas.

4.2   David was _____ mazed to see all the stone fence posts.

4.3   It was dark _____ side the dugout.

4.4   The children did not want to _____ obey Grandmother.

4.5   Judie and Paul walked _____ to the Kirk.

4.6   After the cattle ate the tops, the wheat was still _____ live.

One full truck after another pulled out of the field. Soon the trucks were on their way to town to the elevators.

"Where does the wheat go from the elevator?" asked Paul.

David said, "It goes to the mills that **grind** it into flour. That flour is sent all over the country. People use Red Turkey wheat to make bread."

Read the first sentences. Print the meanings of the words in the blanks.

4.7   At the salt plant, water was evaporated. Water dried up and left salt.
Evaporate means _____.

4.8   The state capital is Topeka.
The city for state business in Kansas is Topeka.
Capital means _____.

4.9   Combines cut and thresh the wheat.
A machine that does several jobs will harvest the wheat.
Combine means _____.

4.10   The geographical center of the parts of the United States that touch is in Kansas. The center of the land of the United States is in Kansas.
Geographical means _____.

DAVID'S OPERATION

Harvest was over. The church held a "Prayer of Thanks" dinner. Everyone thanked God for the good year. Then they said special prayers for David to have a **successful** operation. He would go to the hospital the next day.

Judie and Paul did not see David for a week. They sent letters to him in the hospital.

While they waited for David to come home, they thought about Kansas.

Judie said, "Kansas has so many wonderful things I can't count them."

"God has blessed us. But He has blessed you in Maine, too. You have the ocean. You have forests. You have fishing," said Grandmother.

Soon David was out of the hospital. Judie and Paul rushed to see him.

David was walking on **crutches**. "Does it hurt?" asked Judie. "No," said David, "but I have to use crutches until my knee gets strong."

They enjoyed quiet days together talking about their trip around Kansas.

 **Circle the right answer.**

4.11   Kansas is called the _____ of the nation.
       Breadbasket   Basketball Game   Swimming Pool

4.12   _____ come if there is not enough rain.
       Dust storms   Snowstorms   Rock storms

4.13   One time many _____ came and ate the crops.
       ants   bees   grasshoppers

4.14   Wheat is stored in _____.
       elevators   garages   barns

4.15   Kansas is a(n) _____ name.
       Indian   interesting   useful

4.16   Kansas is in the _____ part of the United States.
       western   center   southern

A BEGINNING AND AN END

Soon the plows came. They looked like **monsters** to Paul and Judie as they turned the soil in the bare wheat fields.

Next came the **disks**. These machines cut the soil in tiny pieces. Round and round they went. Later, the **harrows** came. They made the soil even smoother than the disks had done.

Grandfather said, "Soon we will plant the winter wheat seeds. By spring the field will be green again."

All too soon it was time for Judie and Paul to go home to Maine.

Grandmother, Grandfather, and David went along to the plane.

"I want to go home, but I want to stay, too," said Judie.

"I feel that way, too," said Paul.

They said good-bye to Grandmother and Grandfather. They thanked them for a wonderful summer.

Then Judie and Paul told David they would see him the next summer in Maine. David said, "I'm going to start saving my money right away."

It had been an exciting summer.

Circle the right answer. Print the answer in the blank. Many things happen before you can cut a piece of bread. Use your story to discover when each thing happened.

4.17   The soil is _____ .

      raked   plowed   pounded

4.18   Next the _____ cut the soil into tiny pieces.
        disks   records   platters

4.19   After that the _____ smooth the land.
        harrows   sparrows   wheel barrows

4.20   Winter wheat seeds are planted in _____ .
        winter   fall   spring

4.21   Winter wheat seeds are in the ground during
        the _____ .
        winter   spring   summer

4.22   The seeds start to grow in _____ .
        spring   fall   summer

4.23   Wheat is harvested when it is _____ .
        blue   black   gold

4.24   In summer the _____ cuts and threshes
        the wheat.
        combine   disk   harrow

4.25   Trucks take the wheat to the _____ to be
        stored.
        barn   elevator   storeroom

4.26   Wheat is ground into _____ at the mill.
        flower   flour   floor

Teacher check _____
                    Initial   Date

53 (fifty-three)

Study what you have read and done for this last Self Test. This Self Test will check what you remember in your studies of all parts in this LIFEPAC. The last Self Test will tell you what parts of the LIFEPAC you need to study again.

SELF TEST 4

Write true **or** false.

4.01 _____ Judie and Paul's grandparents live on a Texas farm.

4.02 _____ The Kansas state flower is the sunflower.

4.03 _____ The settlers used wood to make houses.

4.04 _____ Kansas is called the cupboard of America.

4.05 _____ Once grasshoppers ate the farmers' crops.

4.06 _____ When there is no rain in Kansas, dust storms come.

4.07 _____ Combines only cut the wheat.

4.08 _____ Wild animals are kept in game preserves.

4.09 _____ Kansas is known as the Breadbasket of the nation.

Draw lines from the words in the first column to the matching words in the second column.

4.010	combine	cowboy capital
4.011	Kansas	center of the parts of the United States that touch
4.012	Lebanon	state
4.013	dugouts	state flower
4.014	sunflower	machine
4.015	Dodge City	caves

Fill in the blanks of the sentences below with the correct words.

4.016   The _____ grinds wheat into flour.

4.017   Ripe wheat has a _____ color.

4.018   Threshed wheat is stored in _____ .

4.019   Soddies were early houses made of soil and _____ .

4.020   _____ took the wheat to elevators.

4.021   Petroglyphs are _____ writings.

4.022   The capital of Kansas is _____ .

4.023   Strip mining is the way _____ is mined in Kansas.

4.024   The name of one kind of winter wheat is _____ .

4.025   _____ means to bring in the ripe grain.

Teacher check _____

Initial   Date

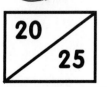

20 / 25

EACH ANSWER, 1 POINT

My Score

Before taking the LIFEPAC Test, you should do these self checks.

1.   Did you do good work on your last Self Test?

2.   Did you study again those parts of the LIFEPAC you didn't remember?

         Check one: ☐ Yes (good)

                            ☐ No (ask your teacher)

3.   Do you know all the new words in "Vocabulary"?

         Check one: ☐ Yes (good)

                            ☐ No (ask your teacher)

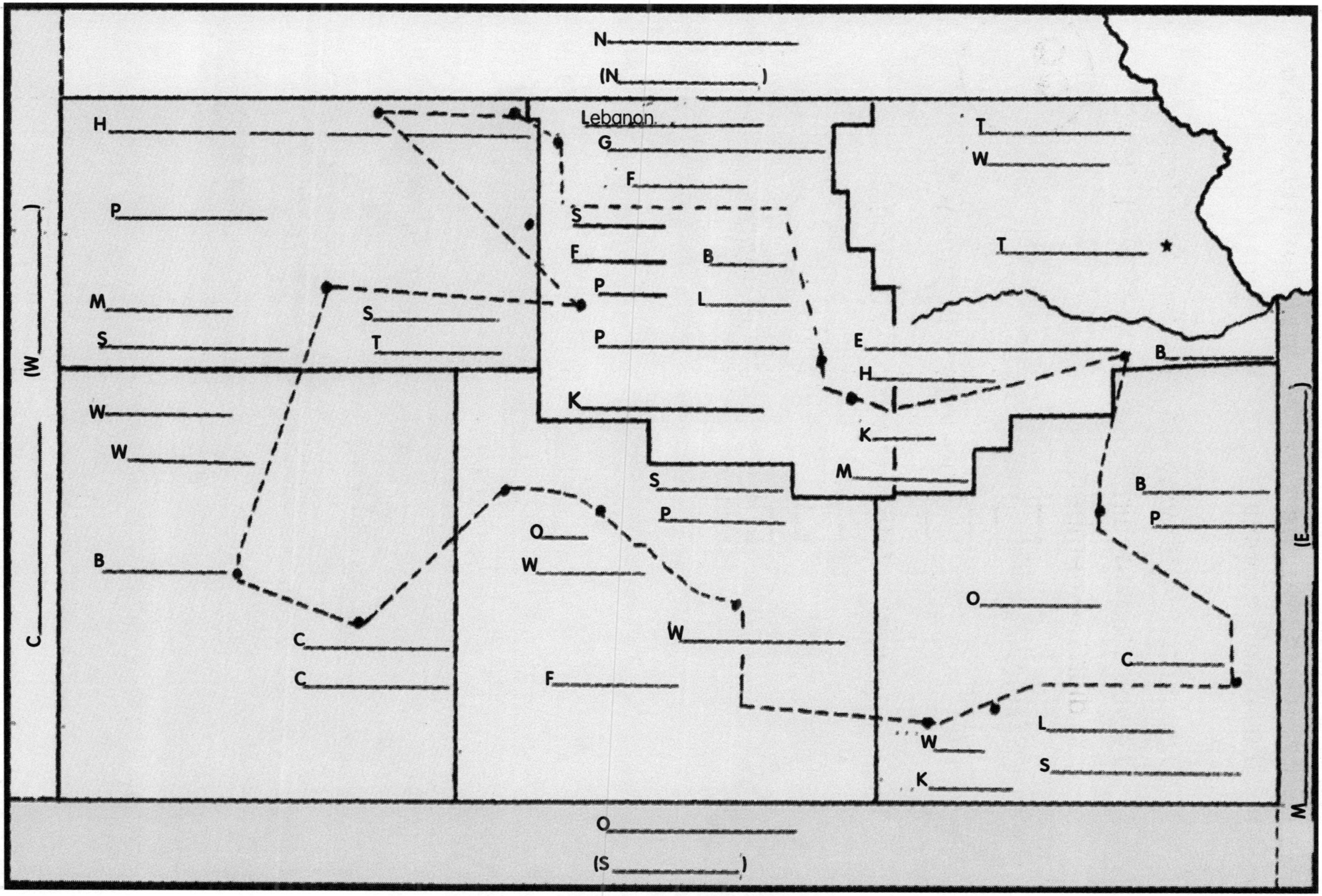

Your Map of Kansas

Lebanon

Your Map of the United States